the
Weekend
Crafter

Etching Glass

the
Weekend
Crafter

Etching Glass

20 Simple, Elegant Projects to Etch with Easy-to-Use Creams and Liquids

PAIGE GILCHRIST AND DIANA LIGHT

LARK BOOKS

A Division of Sterling Publishing Co., Inc.
New York

EDITOR: **PAIGE GILCHRIST**

ART DIRECTOR: **DANA IRWIN**

PHOTOGRAPHY: **SANDRA STAMBAUGH AND RICHARD HASSELBERG**

ILLUSTRATIONS: **HANNES CHAREN**

EDITORAL ASSISTANCE: **HEATHER SMITH**

PRODUCTION ASSISTANCE: **HANNES CHAREN**

Library of Congress Cataloging-in Publication Data

Gilchrist, Paige.
  Etching glass : 20 simple, elegant projects to etch with easy-to-use creams and liquids /
  Paige Gilchrist and Diana Light.
      p. cm. — (The weekend crafter)
Includes index.
ISBN 1-57990-121-2
      1. Glass etching. I. Light, Diana. II. Title. III. Series.

  TT298 .G5497 2000
  748.6'3—dc21   00-030170

10 9 8 7 6 5 4 3 2 1

Published by Lark Books, a division of
Sterling Publishing Co., Inc.
387 Park Avenue South, New York, N.Y. 10016

Distributed in Canada by Sterling Publishing,
c/o Canadian Manda Group, One Atlantic Ave., Suite 105
Toronto, Ontario, Canada M6K 3E7

Distributed in Australia by Capricorn Link (Australia) Pty Ltd., P.O. Box 6651, Baulkham Hills, Business Centre
NSW 2153, Australia

If you have questions or comments about this book, please contact:
Lark Books, 50 College St., Asheville, NC 2880, (828) 253-0467

Manufactured in Hong Kong

ISBN 1-57990-121-2

CONTENTS

Introduction 6

Etching Glass Basics 8

Projects

Monogrammed Decanter & Glasses 20

Starlight Lantern 22

Beaded Necklace 24

Dipped Vase Series 26

Oil Lamp 28

Brushed Platter 30

Room Divider Screen with Mirrors & Frames 32

Stamped Kitchen Jars 34

Wineglasses with Butterflies & Beads 36

Celtic Knot Table 39

Herbed Oil & Vinegar Bottles 42

Snowflake Ornaments 44

Teacups 46

Drawer Pulls 48

Door Frames 50

Breakfast Place Setting 52

Champagne Flutes 55

Hurricane Lamp 58

Punch Bowl Set 60

Martini Set 62

Gallery of Etched Glass 67

Patterns 74

Contributors 78

Acknowledgments 79

Index 80

■ ■ ■

INTRODUCTION

Recently, the humble idea of simplicity has become something of a grand movement. Trouble is, it's awfully easy to stray from the central message. In our headlong rush to pare away the layers in our lives, many of us have loaded up our bookshelves with new guides (one after another after another) that promise to teach us how to cut back, and we've buried ourselves with lists of all we've got to do before we can relax and do less.

If you're nodding your head knowingly but at the same time wondering what any of this has to do with creating frosty, matte designs on pieces of glass, here comes the connection: etching glass is the ultimate simplicity-seeker's craft—and you won't find many books about it.

How can etching glass be so simple? First, it's the opposite of fussy. The process of etching glass with

creams and liquids is as uncomplicated as the clean, elegant results. We'll guide you right past traditional methods for etching glass, which require either specialized abrasive blasting equipment or dangerous acid compounds. Though the results are stunning, the techniques don't lend themselves to quick and easy weekend crafting. With etching creams and liquids, you just choose from a few straightforward methods of applying the etching product to some parts of your glass piece while masking off the other parts. Simply let the product do its quick work and leave it at that,

or, once you've rinsed and dried your etched piece, add a few finishing-touch accents with paints or permanent inks. That's it!

Second, you don't need a whole lot of any kind of paraphernalia. Etching on glass with craft creams and liquids requires only a few purchased products (primarily the cream and/or the liquid) and a handful of everyday tools (we're talking scissors, a ruler, and the like). You've probably already got most of what you need stashed in the drawer where odds and ends collect (thank goodness you haven't yet simplified every nook and cranny!). And, coming up with the glass is simplicity itself—a perfect excuse for using what you already have around the house. We offer designs and techniques for monogramming your cocktail glasses, decorating your drawer pulls, adding etched designs to your windows, and even transforming bottles from the recycling bin into oil lamps.

Finally, etching a piece of glass isn't going to take every spare moment of your free time. (If the idea of scaling back appeals to you, you don't want a hobby that's going to take over your life.) To be frank, this is a fast craft, and the gratification is almost immediate. Transferring designs and cutting out and applying stencils are the most time-consuming parts of the process—and some projects skip those steps entirely. The etching creams and liquids do their work in a matter of 15 minutes or less. After that, you rinse off your glass, and you've got a permanently etched piece.

As far as we know, etching glass hasn't yet been featured by the simplicity gurus as the path to a less complicated and richer life. Why, we wonder? What is this if not the ultimate art of removal, a craft that's about achieving beauty by taking something (in this case, part of the surface of the glass) away?

Life's simplest pleasures are so easily overlooked.

ETCHING GLASS BASICS

Etching Creams and Liquids

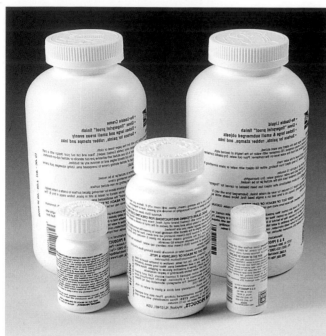

Photo 1: Etching creams and liquids

For more than a hundred years, artists have been etching into the surface of glass using specialized abrasive blasting equipment and dangerous acid compounds. While the results of both methods are spectacular, neither offers home crafters an easy, safe, and inexpensive way to alter the surface of a piece of glass. Now, non-acid etching creams and liquids do.

Based on a relatively safe chemical compound called ammonium bifluoride, etching creams and liquids alter the surface of a piece of glass in a matter of minutes, leaving behind an even, frosted, permanent finish. Various brands of glass-etching products are available at craft-supply stores. Some are reusable; others are not. Some are more environmentally friendly than others. And each may give you slightly different results (you may find some brands work better on large surface areas and others are best for small detail work, for example).

Regardless of which brand you choose, the simple process is the same. You expose the surface of a piece of glass to the cream or liquid (either by spreading or squeezing the cream on or dipping the glass into the liquid). After approximately 15 minutes, every place where the cream or liquid made contact will be permanently etched. Your piece will also be food-and-drink safe and durable enough for the dishwasher.

Resists

Photo 2: Resists, including self-adhesive vinyl and patterns for cutting stencils, purchased stencils, and resist gel

To etch or not to etch—that's where the creativity comes in. Etched glass designs are developed by choosing areas where you want to etch and masking out those that you want protected from the etching process. Anything that does the masking is a *resist*.

Stencils are the most common resists. You can purchase them in craft stores or custom cut your own out of self-adhesive vinyl (the material typically used as shelf paper). The vinyl comes in sheets or rolls and in clear or opaque white. White is easier to work with for most projects, since it doesn't blend in with clear glass. Self-adhesive vinyl also comes with or without a peel-off backing. Be sure to choose a type *with* backing, so you're not dealing with sticky vinyl until you're ready to.

Both standard stencils (a border with cut-out shapes) and reverse stencils (the cut-out shapes themselves) make fine resists, depending on the look you're after. For example, if you cut out a series of stars from a piece of self-adhesive vinyl, then use the sheet as your stencil and etch over it, you end up with a pattern of etched stars. If you use the cut-out stars as your resist instead, you get an etched pattern around un-etched star shapes (see photo 3).

Self-adhesive vinyl can also act as a resist on its own—without a cut-out stencil design. Straight-edged

Photo 3: A project that makes use of both a standard and a reverse stencil

Photo 4: A collection of glass for etching, including flat glass, glasses with simple curves, a hurricane with compound curves, textured glass, glass with raised patterns, and colored glass

strips are perfect for creating open and masked geometric areas, as we did in making the Martini Set on page 62.

Resist gel lets you apply your protective coating in liquid form. You can squeeze out a freehand design directly from an applicator bottle, or you can brush on the gel to mask a larger area. Resist gel works especially well on curved surfaces, where sticking stencils can be a bit more challenging.

Found objects, from leaves to pieces of lace, can all be used as interesting resists. We pressed sprigs of herbs into service on the Herbed Oil & Vinegar Bottles on page 42. Simply use spray adhesive to adhere your object to your piece of glass.

Glass

When you're thinking about glass in terms of its etching ease, it falls into a few broad categories.

Flat Glass. From tabletops and windowpanes to the small panels of glass that cover framed photographs, flat glass is the easiest type to etch if you're using stencils and etching cream. (It's a good choice for any other technique, as well.) Flat glass that you can actually lay flat (as opposed to an installed piece in an upright position) is the easiest of all to etch with stencils.

Glass with Simple Curves. Pieces with single curves, such as standard drinking glasses or cylindrical vases, aren't quite as effortless to work on as flat glass, but they're a fine choice for stencils and etching cream—or for any other etching technique.

Word to the Wise

Plastic masquerading as glass won't ever stand up to etching, so shop carefully. If you're stumped about whether a piece is lightweight glass or plastic, tap it and listen for the telltale ring—or ask a sales clerk to verify that it's glass.

Glass with Compound Curves. If a piece of glass has both horizontal and vertical curves (a wine glass is the most common example), getting a stencil to lie flat on the surface will require some maneuvering (and strategic snipping), but it's certainly possible. Easier options for glass with compound curves include applying etching cream directly from an applicator bottle or dipping the glass in etching liquid.

Textured Glass. Stencils may not stick well to a piece of glass with a textured or uneven surface. Your best bet when working with textured glass is to dip it in etching liquid or apply a freehand design of etching cream with an applicator bottle.

Glass with a Raised Pattern. Much of your design work is already done if you've got a piece of glass with a raised pattern, whether it's the letters and logo on an old milk bottle or a floral motif on a set of salad plates. You can simply trace the pattern with etching cream squeezed from an applicator bottle to make it appear as if it was etched into the glass all along.

Colored Glass. Colored glass will etch just as beautifully as clear glass—as long as it's really colored and not color coated. In many cases, color-coated glass can be etched, too, but it's best to test a piece first to be sure (try a small, inconspicuous spot on the bottom of the object). Occasionally, when you're working with color-coated glass, the fumes will eat off a small area of the coating near where you etched. There's also the chance that your stencil will pull part of the coating up with it when you remove it.

Etching Supplies

SQUEEGEE

A flexible, T-shaped or rectangular plastic tool comes in handy at various stages in the etching process. If you're applying an adhesive stencil to your piece of glass, a squeegee is a perfect little paddle for smoothing it on and rubbing it firmly in place, making sure there are no wrinkles, air bubbles, or insecure edges where etching cream could seep underneath. It's also just what you need for spreading and smoothing etching cream over the surface you want etched, and for scraping reusable brands of cream back into their containers afterward.

APPLICATOR BOTTLES & TIPS

At times, you may want to apply etching cream or resist gel to your glass by "drawing" it on freehand, much the same way you'd squeeze icing onto a cake. If so, you'll need applicator bottles for the cream or gel and an assortment of changeable tips that let you switch from bold, thick lines to delicate skinny ones (or some size in between) quickly and easily.

Photo 5: Glass etching supplies

To clean a tip after using it, attach it to a bottle filled with warm water, and squeeze the water through the tip. A straight pin or needle will unblock a tip that gets clogged in the process.

CRAFT KNIFE & BLADES

Since cutting out stencils can be a big part of the glass-etching process, a good craft knife and a supply of sharp blades are essential. Use swivel blades, which rotate 360° when you hold them upright, for cutting smooth, even edges on stencils with curves and rounded shapes. They work best when you're cutting out a stencil that has already been applied to the glass. Classic fine-point #11 blades work well for cutting straight lines in stencils that are either on or off the glass. Specially designed pick-out tools, sharp only at the tip, are best for carefully remov-

Photo 6: Materials and supplies for embellishing etched glass pieces

ing the inner parts of stencils without destroying the clean edges around them. You can also use your fine-point #11 blade for removing the inner parts of stencils.

SCISSORS

For cutting out some stencils, good old-fashioned scissors work best. The leaf shapes for the Hurricane Lamp on page 58 are a good example.

RULER

This trusty craft tool comes in handy at various times. You'll use it anytime you want to draw straight lines as a part of a stencil or mark lines directly onto your glass (if you're masking out geometric areas, for example). A ruler will also help you position your stencil on your glass when you're centering it or placing it in some other specific way. And it's a great cutting guide.

SAFETY EQUIPMENT

Though you don't need to take heavy precautions when working with etching creams, liquids, and gels, it's good to keep in mind that you are dealing with chemicals. Slip on some latex gloves if your fingers are going to come in contact with the product, and always work in a well-ventilated area. Safety glasses are a good idea for times when splattering is a possibility (such as when you're dropping glass objects into etching liquid or rinsing cream off of finished pieces). If you plan to be working with the products for several days in a row and/or for long stretches of time, consider a mask for your nose and mouth.

OTHER SUPPLIES

You'll also need a clear plastic container and a water-based permanent marker or china marker if you're using etching liquid (see Techniques), a wooden or plastic spoon for stirring your etching cream before using it (because wooden spoons are porous, don't use them with food after stirring etching cream with them), a timer or clock to time the etching process, and water and a sponge to clean your pieces after they're etched. An inexpensive cutting board comes in handy, too. It's a good surface for cutting out stencils. And, if you set a piece you're etching on top of it, you can easily rotate it as you work by turning the cutting board.

Techniques

MAKING STENCILS

You can transfer your own designs, any of the patterns provided in this book, or other patterns you like to self-adhesive vinyl to create your own stencils. First, make sure the design or pattern is the size you want (reduce or enlarge it on a copy machine, if necessary). Next, lay the self-adhesive vinyl flat (with the side with adhesive backing facing down), lay a piece of carbon paper on top of it (carbon side down), and lay your design or pattern on top of that. It's a good idea to tape all the pieces together so they stay in place while you transfer. Finally, use a ballpoint pen to trace around the image (see photo 7). When you finish, you'll have a transferred carbon version of the image on top of the self-adhesive vinyl.

Photo 7: Transferring a pattern to self-adhesive vinyl

Tip

When you're choosing designs for stencils, stay away from those that have lots of single, thin lines as a part of the design. They'll be difficult to cut out cleanly, and they may not translate well as an etched image.

CUTTING OUT STENCILS

You've got two choices for cutting out your stencils. You can either make the cuts before you apply the stencils to your glass, or you can apply the piece of self-adhesive paper on which the stencil design appears, then cut out your stencil once it's in place on the glass.

Deciding which way seems easiest is really a case-by-case job, but here are some general guidelines.

- Cut out the stencil before applying it to the glass (see photo 8) if you want to save the pieces you're cutting out to use as resists for another piece of glass. The Starlight Lantern project (page 22) is a good example. The star shapes you cut out to create a stencil for one panel of the lantern become reverse stencils for the next panel. Therefore, both need to be cut out while their adhesive backing is still in place (in other words, before the self-adhesive vinyl has been applied to the glass). You'll also want to cut out your stencil before applying it when you need to see through the cut design to accurately place it on the glass, as you do with the Stamped Kitchen Jars on page 34.

Photo 8: Cutting out a stencil before applying it to the glass

- Cut out the stencil after you've applied the self-adhesive vinyl to the glass (see photo 9) if the stencil has lots of intricate curves you want to cut out with a swivel blade.

Photo 9: Cutting out a stencil on the glass

Photo 10: Remove pieces of your stencil by picking them out from the center rather than by working from the edge.

(Swivel blades work best once the stencil is already on the glass, because then they don't have to cut through the layer of backing in addition to the vinyl.) Also, if your design is quite large (the one for the Celtic Knot Table on page 39 is a good example), a precut stencil could be too unwieldy to apply to the glass surface. Better to cut it out once the self-adhesive vinyl is already on the glass.

Regardless of whether you're cutting out your stencil before or after you apply it to the glass, be careful not to cut too far at places where lines meet (such as at the corners of a square or the points of a star). See figure 1. If you cut beyond where the lines meet, you'll create a small slit in the stencil where etching cream can seep into an area you meant to keep protected. In addition, carefully remove the pieces of your stencil you've cut out by using a fine-point #11 blade in your craft knife or a specially designed picking tool to pick the piece out from its center (see photo 10). If you work from the edge of the piece instead, you risk destroying the clean lines you've cut.

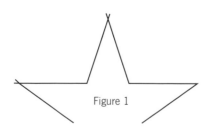

Figure 1

APPLYING STENCILS AND OTHER RESISTS

Before applying anything, make sure your glass is clean, checking for lint, oil, and residue from any adhesive price stickers.

Stencils

The process for applying stencils is the same, whether you cut them out before applying them or after.

1. Start to peel off the stencil's adhesive backing.

2. Begin laying down the stencil, starting from one side and smoothing down the self-adhesive vinyl with your hand or the squeegee as you move to the other side (see photo 11).

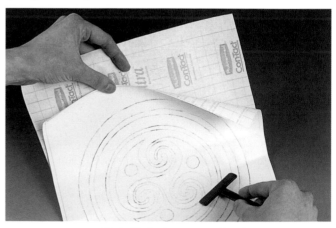

Photo 11: Applying a stencil to glass

3. Place the backing you peeled off in step 1 on top of the stencil and use the squeegee to press the stencil firmly in place, making sure all edges have a good grip on the glass. (Without the adhesive backing as a buffer, you might accidentally push edges up rather than press them in place. If you cut the stencil out before applying it, you'll need an uncut scrap of adhesive backing from another project to use as your buffer.)

4. Rub off any adhesive residue from the self-adhesive vinyl with your fingers or with a very lightly moistened cotton swab, being careful not to get any moisture under the vinyl. Once you've applied your stencil, etch your glass as soon as possible. The longer the stencil stays in place, the harder it will be to remove when you're finished.

Tip

If you're applying a stencil to a curved surface, you'll probably need to use a craft knife or scissors to cut fringe around the edges of the piece of self-adhesive vinyl so it will lie down smoothly over the contours in the glass.

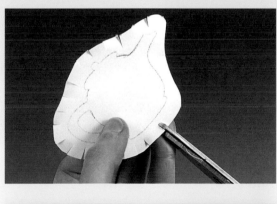

Found Object Resists

All it takes is a thin coating of spray adhesive to attach a found object to your glass. As with vinyl stencils, you want to make sure whatever you're sticking on is firmly in place so that etching cream won't seep underneath. Cover your attached found object with a scrap piece of vinyl backing, then use the squeegee to carefully secure the bond.

Self-Adhesive Vinyl Resists

Laying down strips of self-adhesive vinyl to serve as solid patches of resist is much like applying a stencil. However, it's more likely with this method that you'll have overlapping pieces of self-adhesive paper. Be sure to use a blunt tool or your fingernail to burnish the seams when you do (see photo 12), or etching cream or liquid may seep underneath them.

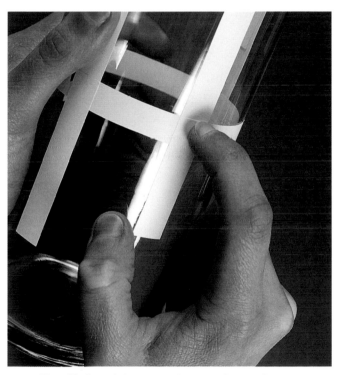

Photo 12: Burnish the seams where stencil material meets.

You can also use self-adhesive vinyl to create extension strips around a stencil to protect the surrounding glass from the etching product (see photo 13). And, if you plan to etch the outside of a glass but want the inside to remain clear, you'll need a strip of self-adhesive vinyl measuring 1 inch (2.5 cm) or more along the inside rim of the object (see photo 14).

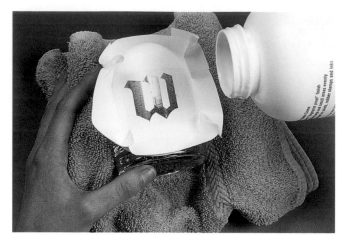

Photo 13: You can use self-adhesive vinyl to create extension strips around a stencil area before applying etching cream.

Photo 14: Using self-adhesive vinyl to protect the inside rim of a glass

Resist Gel

Before applying resist gel, experiment with it on a sheet of paper to make sure the applicator tip you're using gives you the line size you want. The consistency of resist gel doesn't match that of etching cream, so the results you get with applicator tips will be different depending on the product you're using. Once you're satisfied with your line size, you can start squeezing the gel onto your glass, just as if you were squeezing icing from a tube. Resist gel is great for stippling on dots (as we did on some of the beads in the Beaded Necklace on page 24). It's also perfect for swirls, squiggles, and hard-to-stencil objects, like the Drawer Pulls on page 48. Best of all, it's forgiving. If you squeeze a bit where you don't want it, you can wash it off and start over. Wait until the resist gel dries clear (this can take minutes to hours, depending on how thickly you applied the gel) before etching over it. A hair dryer is the best way to speed up the process if patience isn't one of your virtues.

APPLYING ETCHING CREAM

With a Squeegee

If you pour etching cream directly onto the areas you want etched, it may take effect unevenly, causing the glass to etch in a ripple-type fashion. Pulling the cream smoothly across the exposed glass areas solves the problem.

1. Stir the etching cream well before you begin. (Cream that hasn't been stirred well can also produce an uneven etch.) Pour a generous amount onto an unexposed section of your stencil.

Building a Well

If you're etching with cream on a curved surface, you need a way to keep the cream contained, so it doesn't spread beyond the area you want to etch. The same self-adhesive vinyl you used to make your stencil does the trick. Cut strips 1 to 2 inches wide (2.5 to 5 cm), lay them down around the edges of the stencil, then pinch them together where they meet to build up a protective well around the etching area.

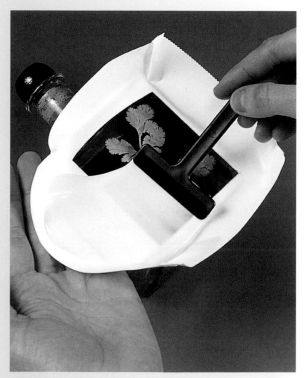

Creating a well around a stencil area to protect the rest of the glass from etching cream

2. Use a squeegee to pull the cream evenly and thickly across the exposed area (see photo 15). (Don't be tempted to use a brush instead of a squeegee. Brushes won't spread the cream smoothly, and they can cause streaking.)

Photo 15: Pulling etching cream over a stencil area with a squeegee

3. Leave the cream on for approximately 15 minutes (follow your cream manufacturer's directions for the exact amount of time). When the time is up, scrape it off the glass surface. (If your cream is reusable, scrape it right back into its container.)

4. Rinse the glass with water to remove the stencil and any remaining cream. Water is the critical ingredient here; it stops the etching action and prevents the cream from affecting other areas of the glass. Most important at this stage, don't despair when you don't see your etched design! It won't show up until you dry the glass well. Once you do, your permanently etched image will emerge.

With an Applicator Bottle

When you'd rather not mess with cutting and sticking stencils, you can squeeze etching cream straight from an applicator bottle. Both metal and plastic applicator tips come in a variety of sizes, so you can tailor the thickness of the image you etch to the size of the piece you're working on. Practice first on a piece of paper to make sure the tip you've chosen gives you the results you want. The cream

starts etching the minute it comes in contact with the glass, so you can't wipe it off and try another tip once you've started. You can squeeze cream from an applicator bottle to trace a raised pattern in a piece of glass (see the Punch Bowl Set on page 60), create tiny circles for bubbles or dots, or quickly personalize glass gifts, from wine bottles to flower vases, with freehand squiggles, swirls, or lettering.

With a Sponge

Perhaps it's not a classic glass-etching technique, but if you want a little texture, sponging works. It's also a good way to cover a large surface full of compound curves (see the Hurricane Lamp, page 58). Play with foam sponges, kitchen sponges, cosmetic sponges, and sea sponges to get a feel for the variety of effects you can create. When you're ready to etch, pour the cream into a plastic lid, load a dry sponge (water will prevent the cream from working), and sponge your glass surface using a straight up-and-down motion (as opposed to using the sponge to smear the cream). The thicker you sponge, the more solidly white your etched area will be.

With a Brush

Though you should stay away from paintbrushes if your goal is to apply an even layer of etching cream, they can be used to achieve a less traditional etched look. The simple, fan-shaped flower petals on the Brushed Platter, page 30, are a good example. Etching cream is going to be rougher on your brushes than paint, so just be sure you don't use your all-time favorite (or most expensive) one.

DIPPING WITH ETCHING LIQUID

Dipping can be as effortless as it sounds. If you've got something you want to evenly etch all over (a bead, for example), simply drop it in a bit of etching liquid, let it sit for the period of time the manufacturer recommends (about 15 minutes, typically), then lift it out, rinse it, and dry it.

Pieces you want only partially etched call for a little measuring. Say you want a vase etched only partway up. Stand one of the vases in a clear plastic container, fill it with water up to the point where you want the etching to stop, then remove the vase (see photo 16). The water level will drop without the vase in the container taking up space. With a water-based marker or a china marker, make a line to note the water level on the outside of the

Photo 16: Determining the level for etching liquid

EMBELLISHING

In addition to giving your glass an elegant, frosted appearance, the etching process creates a textured surface perfect for painting or stamping if you want to add color or a bit more design.

Any acrylic or oil paint will grab hold and cure on top of an etched surface. Or, you can use new, widely available paints developed especially for painting on glass. They come in opaque and transparent varieties in bottles, squeeze tubes, and as paint pens. Glass paints will adhere to both etched and unetched surfaces, and many are dishwasher safe (and some are even food safe) after you bake them in the oven for 30 minutes to "fire" them. You can also use rubber stamps with either permanent ink or embossing powders to transfer complete images to your etched piece.

container (see photo 17). Pour the water out of the container, dry the container and the outside of the vase well, then fill the container with etching liquid up to the line you marked. Set your vase into the liquid to etch, placing it slowly and carefully to avoid any splashing. Be sure you're working on a flat, level surface, or your etch line will be slanted, and don't move the piece once it's settled.

An air bubble will develop under any piece of glass with a bottom (a piece of stemware or a bottle, for

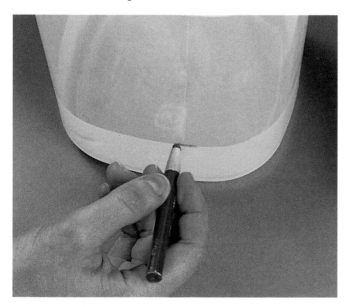

Photo 17: Marking a line for etching liquid

instance), causing a small, unetched spot. If you want to fill it in once the rest of the piece is finished, put on latex gloves and apply a small amount of etching cream with your finger, leave it on for about five minutes, then rinse and dry the spot.

PROTECTING WHAT YOU DON'T WANT ETCHED

Most etching products work not only on glass and mirrors, but on ceramics, porcelain, and marble as well, which means you'll want to keep the cream and liquid away from objects made of these materials if you don't want them etched. Don't use a glass container for liquid dipping, for example. And use a sink other than a porcelain one for rinsing cream off your finished pieces. Etching liquid and cream can also discolor stainless steel flatware and sinks. Be sure to wash any utensils you use immediately after they've come in contact with the products, and don't leave spots of cream sitting in your sink.

Photo 18: Large etched squares serve as canvases for a series of rubber-stamped tree images.

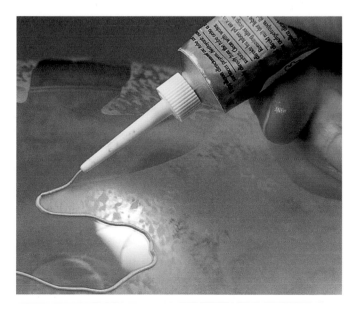

Photo 19: Using paints designed for glass on top of an etched image

Photo 20: Outlining an etched image with outliner paste, designed for painting on glass

Monogrammed Decanter and Glasses

So, you didn't inherit a collection of heirloom glasses etched with the family initials and crest. No need to cancel the cocktail party. Pre-made monogram stencils are widely available, making a stunning set like this unbelievably easy to etch.

Decanter and glasses

Purchased monogram stencil in letter or letters of your choice (You can reuse the same stencil for each piece by applying it with adhesive spray.)

Adhesive spray (optional)

Scrap piece of self-adhesive vinyl backing

Squeegee

Craft knife or scissors

Cotton swabs (optional)

Self-adhesive vinyl

Towel

Etching cream

Utensil for stirring etching cream

1 Center your stencil and apply it to your first piece of glass. (If it's not a self-adhesive stencil, use adhesive spray to apply it.) Cover the stencil with backing from a piece of self-adhesive vinyl, and squeegee over it to make sure the stencil is firmly in place.

2 Rub off any adhesive residue that you pushed out onto the glass in step 1 with your fingers or with a slightly moistened cotton swab.

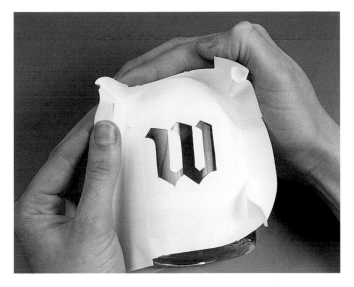

3 Add strips of self-adhesive vinyl around the stencil, and pinch them together at the corners to form a well that will prevent the etching cream from flowing onto the rest of the glass.

4 Nestle the glass in a towel so it won't roll. Stir the etching cream, pour it onto one of the vinyl strips along the edge of the stencil, and use the squeegee to pull it quickly and evenly across the stencil. Leave the cream in place for the amount of time the manufacturer recommends. Scrape off the excess cream with the squeegee, and remove the stencil as you rinse the glass with water. Dry the glass, then repeat steps 1 through 4 with the other pieces in your set.

Starlight Lantern

This project makes the most of a single stencil pattern. First, a standard stencil scatters etched stars all over one panel of your lantern. Then, the cutout shapes from the first stencil become reverse stencils, creating clear stars floating on an etched background on the next panel. Repeat the alternating process until all the panels are etched, and you've got an outdoor lantern that twinkles.

WHAT YOU NEED

Lantern with an even number of multiple glass panels

Starlight Lantern stencil pattern, page 74, sized on a photocopy machine to fit the panels of your lantern

Self-adhesive vinyl

Carbon paper

Ballpoint pen

Craft knife

Ruler

Etching cream

Squeegee

Scraps of self-adhesive vinyl backing leftover from another project

Tape

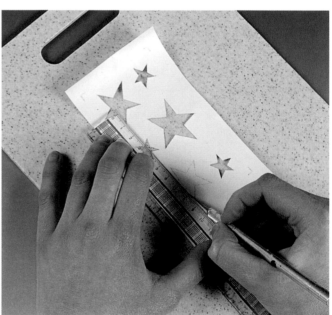

1 Transfer your sized pattern to self-adhesive vinyl (once for every two panels in your lantern), using carbon paper and a ballpoint pen. Mark the corners of the stencils according to the measurements of your lantern's panels, then leave a border of self-adhesive vinyl measuring 1½ to 2 inches (3.8 to 5 cm) beyond the marked corners. With a sharp new blade in your craft knife, cut out the star shapes in each stencil, being careful not to overcut at any of the points on the star. (Remember, you'll be using both the star shapes and the standard stencil; both need to be cleanly cut.)

2 Begin peeling off the self-adhesive vinyl backing on one end of the stencil, and position that end on one of the lantern panels, using the corners you marked in step 1 as a guide. Once you're sure of the stencil's position, continue peeling off the backing, and use the squeegee to guide the stencil into position. To press the stencil firmly in place and remove any air bubbles, cover it with a scrap of self-adhesive vinyl backing and run the squeegee over it.

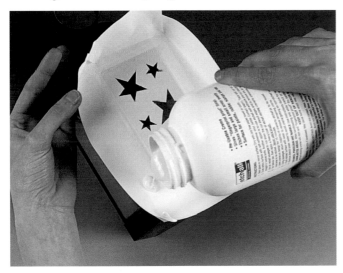

3 Wipe off any adhesive residue the vinyl may have left on the glass. Add extension strips of self-adhesive vinyl around the stencil's border, then pinch the strips at the corners to make a well for the etching cream. Pour a small amount of cream into the well, and pull it smoothly over the stencil area with the squeegee. Leave the cream in place for the amount of time the cream manufacturer recommends, scrape it off, and remove the stencil as you rinse the panel with water. Dry the panel.

4 On the next panel, stick on the stars you cut out to create the stencil, using the stencil as a guide for positioning them. Cover the panel with a scrap of self-adhesive vinyl backing, and run the squeegee over the stars to remove any air bubbles and ensure that they're firmly in place. Wipe off any adhesive residue on the glass.

5 Cut a strip of self-adhesive vinyl a bit longer than the panel and approximately 1½ to 2 inches (3.8 to 5 cm) wide, and attach it to one side of the panel you're about to etch (attaching the vinyl to the lantern material rather than the glass). Pour a line of etching cream onto the strip, and pull it smoothly over the stencil area with the squeegee. Leave the cream in place for the amount of time the cream manufacturer recommends, scrape it off, and remove the stars as you rinse the panel with water. Dry the panel. Repeat the alternating process on all of the lantern's remaining panels.

Beaded Necklace

Bead shops have aisles full of irresistible glass beads you can string together into a necklace or bracelet yourself. And, of course, any place that carries jewelry will sell you what you're looking for already strung and ready to wear. Your beads will look fine, draped around your neck or dangling from your wrist, just the way they are. But giving them the added allure of an etched design is so simple, you may never wear clear glass again.

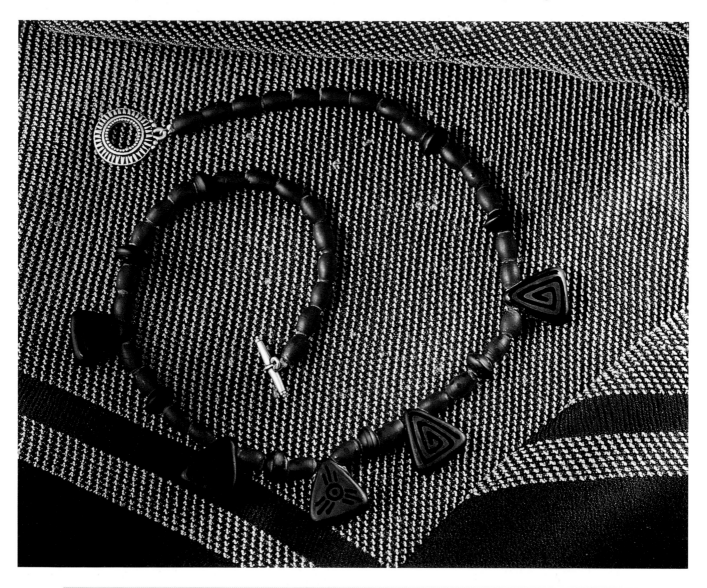

WHAT YOU NEED

Scrap paper	Etching liquid
Pen or pencil (optional)	Plastic container
Necklace made of glass beads	Safety glasses
Resist gel in applicator bottle with smallest tip available	Plastic or wooden spoon

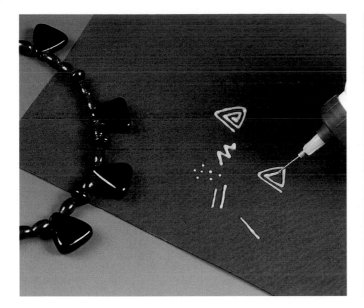

1 If you like, sketch simple designs for your beads on a piece of paper first, or use the designs on page 74 as a guide. You'll also want to test the tip on your applicator bottle to make sure it produces a line of resist gel that is thin enough to work on your bead surfaces. While doing so, practice drawing your designs with the resist gel.

2 Once you're satisfied with your designs, begin drawing them on the beads with the resist gel.

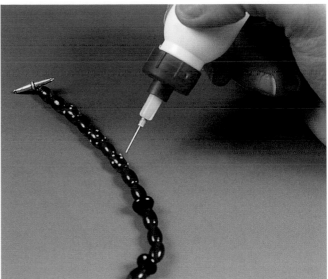

3 Very simple designs, such as the dots we're applying here, work best on small beads. To apply the gel to all sides of round beads, hold the necklace up in the air or suspend it from a hook that will allow it to dangle freely. Once you're finished, hang the necklace and let the resist gel dry until it's clear.

4 Wearing safety glasses, pour enough etching liquid into the plastic container to cover the necklace. Place the necklace into the liquid, and gently move it with the plastic or wooden spoon to ensure good coverage of all the beads. After the amount of time the etching liquid manufacturer recommends, pour off the liquid (pouring it back into its original container if it's reusable), rinse the necklace and wipe off the gel, and dry it.

Dipped Vase Series

Place a graceful set like this one on a mantel or in the middle of a table, and it doubles as a piece of minimalist art. But what's really minimal is the amount of work required to make it. The simple process involves nothing more than dipping one bud vase after another in a different level of etching liquid.

WHAT YOU NEED

Collection of vases	Safety glasses
Plastic container	Etching cream
Water	Utensil for stirring etching cream
Water-based marker or china marker	Latex gloves
Etching liquid	

1 Fill the vases with water to give them additional weight. Put one vase in the plastic container, and fill the container with water until the waterline reaches the point on the vase where you want your lowest etch line to be.

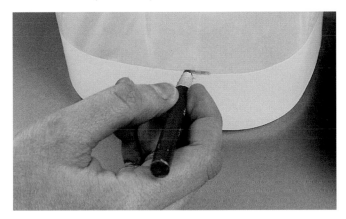

2 Remove the vase, and mark the water level on the container with the water-based marker or china marker. Repeat the process to mark the water level for your highest etch line. Then, make evenly spaced marks for as many levels as you want in between your highest and lowest levels. (For this project, for example, we were working with seven vases, so after marking the highest and lowest etching levels, we marked five evenly spaced levels in between.)

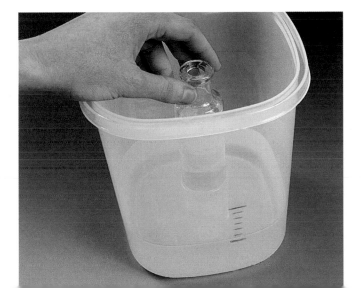

3 Dump out the water from the plastic container (leave the water in the vase) and dry the container and the outside of the vase thoroughly. Working on a level surface and wearing safety glasses to protect your eyes from any splashing, pour etching liquid into the container up to the lowest marked level. Slowly place your first vase into the liquid, being careful to lower it in a perfectly upright position. The etching liquid begins to work immediately, so tilting the bottle could cause an uneven etch. Allow the vase to sit in the liquid for the amount of time the manufacturer recommends.

4 Remove the first vase, and rinse and dry it. Repeat the process for the other vases in your collection, using the marks you made to increase the level of etching liquid by one increment for each vase. (Be sure to add the etching liquid before placing your vase in the plastic container each time.) When you finish, if the etching liquid is reusable, pour it back into its original container.

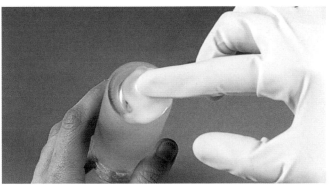

5 Finish the bottom of each vase (where air prevented the liquid from etching), by applying a bit of etching creme with a gloved finger. Stir the etching cream well before applying it, leave it on for approximately five minutes, then rinse and dry the bottom of each vase.

Oil Lamp

Here's a nod to the adage that opposites attract. You've got a rigid row of etched tapers below, frosty looking and firmly in place. Illuminating them from above is a warm, flickering flame. This project shows you how to bottle your own brand of contrast.

WHAT YOU NEED

Oil Lamp stencil pattern, page 74, sized on a photocopy machine to fit the surface you want to etch

Carbon paper

Ballpoint pen

Self-adhesive vinyl

Craft knife with a straight blade and a swivel blade (optional)

Pick-out tool (optional)

Ruler

Bottle

Squeegee

Cotton swabs
(optional)

Etching cream

Utensil for stirring etching cream

Lamp oil

Wick

NOTE

We used an assortment of old and recycled bottles for the oil lamps shown here. Older bottles make lamps with appealing character, but their weathered surfaces may retain quite a bit of residue from the self-adhesive vinyl. To reduce residue cleanup, don't place the stencil on the bottle until right before you're ready to etch, then remove it as soon as the etching cream has taken effect.

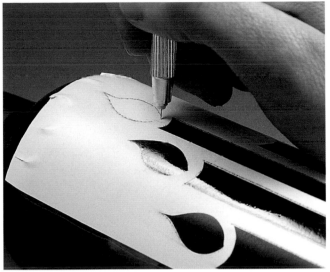

1 Transfer your sized stencil pattern to a piece of self-adhesive vinyl. With a straight blade and a ruler, cut out the straight candle pieces of the stencil.

3 Once the stencil is in place on the bottle, cut out the flame pieces. A swivel blade works best for cutting out the shapes. Then, use a straight blade or a pick-out tool to pick the pieces out of the stencil, working from the center of the piece you're removing, not the edges. Once all of the pieces are removed, cover the stencil with a piece of self-adhesive vinyl backing and squeegee over it to press it firmly in place. Remove any adhesive residue from the glass with your fingers

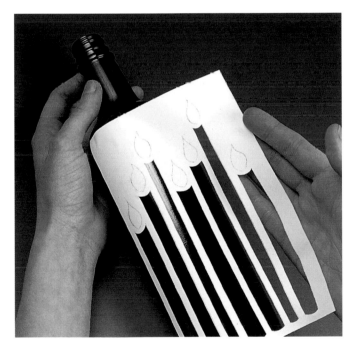

2 Apply the stencil to your bottle. If you're working on a bottle with a flat surface, mark corners around the stencil design first that correspond with the corners of the bottle's surface, then use those corners to center the stencil on the bottle. If you're working on a round bottle, line up the straight edge of your stencil with the seam on the side of the bottle.

4 Add strips of self-adhesive vinyl around the edges of the stencil and, if you're working on a rounded bottle, make a well to contain the etching cream. Stir the cream, pour it onto one of the vinyl edges, and spread it quickly and evenly over the entire stencil with the squeegee. Leave it in place for the amount of time the manufacturer recommends, then scrape off the excess cream with the squeegee, and remove the stencil as you rinse the bottle with water. Dry the bottle, and add lamp oil and a wick.

Brushed Platter

Some days, the clean, clear lines of a carefully cut stencil seem a little too confining. You crave the free-form appeal of a brush stroke. Painting isn't a technique that's often used with etching cream, but this simple design pairs the two beautifully.

Brushed Platter pattern on page 74, sized on a photocopy machine to fit your platter

Platter

Dry artist's brush (medium round)

Etching cream

Utensil for stirring etching cream

Flat plastic dish or lid

Applicator bottle filled with etching cream and equipped with a small tip

3 Continue pressing fan-shaped petals onto the platter, three per flower, following the guide underneath the platter. Be careful not to smear the cream as you apply it.

1 Use the pattern on page 74 as a guide for placement of your flowers, or sketch out a placement design of your own. Turn your platter upside down and put it on top of the pattern.

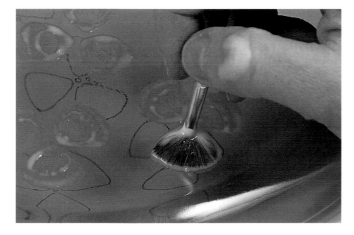

2 Stir the etching cream and pour some into the plastic dish or lid, dip your brush in and load it with a medium amount of cream, and press it down at an angle on the platter (over one of the petal guides), creating a fan shape with the bristles. You want to be sure the brush is full of cream but not so saturated that you can't create a clean petal image. Lift the brush straight up after creating each petal mark.

4 Use the applicator bottle to apply three dots in the center of each flower, again following the pattern as a guide. Leave the cream in place for the amount of time the manufacturer recommends, then rinse the platter with water and dry it.

Room Divider Screen with Mirrors & Frames

Don't be daunted by the showy finished product; this is actually one of the most beginner-friendly projects in the book! It's just a simple design of curved lines and dots applied to flat glass panels and mirrors that are then inserted into a screen. It's also a project you can scale way down. If you don't happen to have a screen like this one handy, you can still etch the easy cherry blossom design on any mirror or glass-paneled picture frame.

Room divider screen designed to display photographs

Glass and mirror panels (mirror panels optional) cut to fit slots in screen (If your screen comes with plastic panels, as ours did, a glass-and-mirror supplier can easily cut replacement panels for a nominal fee.)

Both versions of the Room Divider Screen pattern, page 75, sized on a photocopy machine to fit your glass panels (Be sure to size the patterns to fit only the area of your panels that will be exposed. Remember that part of the panels will be covered by the lip of the frame.)

Etching cream in applicator bottle with medium tip

3 Apply the flower dots, making sure you leave enough space between each so they don't run together.

1 Center one version of your pattern under one of the glass panels. We've provided two versions of the pattern so that you can position one to make the cherry blossom branch extend from your panel's upper-left corner or lower-right corner, and the other to make the branch extend from the upper-right corner or lower-left corner. If you're etching a group of glass panels that will be displayed together in a screen like this one (or in some other grouping), map out ahead of time how you want the design positioned on each panel. When you do so, keep in mind that you'll probably want to etch what will be the back side of the glass panel, so that the design has added depth and the front of the panel will be easier to clean.

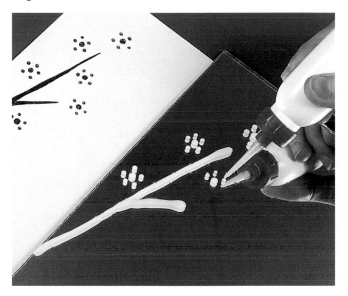

4 Once you've traced this simple pattern on several glass panels, you'll be familiar enough with it to squeeze out a freehand version on mirror panels, if you wish. Leave the cream in place for the amount of time the manufacturer recommends, then rinse the panels with water, dry them, and position them in the screen, with photographs behind the glass panels.

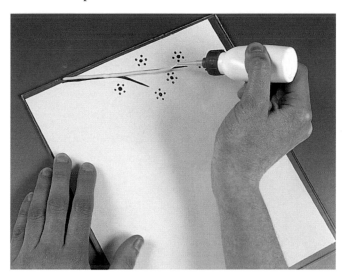

2 Squeeze the etching cream onto the glass, following the lines of the pattern underneath. Work on the branches first.

Stamped Kitchen Jars

The allure of stamping is that you can add ink to almost anything (from leaves and fabric scraps to that trusty standby, carved potatoes), press the inked object onto a surface, and you've got a printed image. Of course, purchased rubber stamps work well, too. And a simple etched background provides just the surface you need to apply your stamp to a panel of glass.

WHAT YOU NEED

Square glass jars	Etching cream
Ruler	Utensil for stirring etching cream
Plain paper	Squeegee
Ballpoint pen	Rubber stamp(s) (We used four different seasonal tree images for our jars.)
Self-adhesive vinyl	
Carbon paper	Permanent, water-resistant ink and dry ink pad
Craft knife or scissors	Mineral spirits or stamp cleaner (optional)
Tape	Fine-point artist's brush (optional)

1 Determine how large a square you want to etch on your jars' panels. Be sure it's slightly larger than the stamp(s) you've chosen. (Ours measures 2¼ inches [5.7 cm] square.) Draw your square stencil on the plain sheet of paper, transfer four copies per jar to self-adhesive vinyl, leaving a border of approximately 2 inches (5 cm) around each, and cut them out. Take care not to overcut at the corners; if you do, you'll create slits in the stencil where etching cream could seep in.

2 Tape one of the squares that you cut from the center of a stencil to an inside panel of one of the jars, positioning it exactly where you want your etched square to appear.

3 Lay the jar on one of its sides (the opposite one from where you taped the square). Using the taped square as a guide, apply one of the stencils to the outside of the jar panel, then remove the square taped on the inside of the jar.

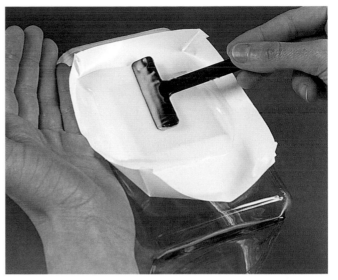

4 Stir the etching cream well, then pour a small puddle onto the vinyl, and use the squeegee to pull it quickly and evenly across the square opening. Leave the cream in place for the amount of time the manufacturer recommends, scrape it off with the squeegee, then remove the vinyl stencil as you rinse the jar with water. Dry the jar, and repeat steps 2 through 4 on all of your other jar panels.

5 Saturate your ink pad with ink. Ink your stamp, then press the image in place in the center of each of your jars' etched panels. If the panels are not completely flat, making it difficult to transfer an even stamped image, pull your stamp off of its wooden handle, so you've got a more flexible piece to press into place. You can also use a fine-point artist's brush dipped in ink to fill in any small areas where the image didn't transfer well. Mineral spirits will clean up any mistakes—or remove the entire stamped image while it's still wet, if you decide you want to start over.

Wineglasses with Butterflies & Beads

If single-technique projects leave you longing for a bit more action, here's one that offers just the variety you've been craving. You'll start by creating a stencil and covering it with etching cream, move on to dipping beads in etching liquid, and finish up by adding a flourish of wrapped wire. Best of all, it's easy to personalize the look of these gift-worthy glasses each time you create a new set by choosing different glass colors and bead styles.

WHAT YOU NEED

Wineglasses

Wineglasses with Butterflies & Beads stencil pattern, page 75, sized on a photocopy machine to fit your glasses

Carbon paper

Ballpoint pen

Self-adhesive vinyl

Craft knife with a swivel blade and a straight blade

Pick-out tool (optional)

Cotton swabs (optional)

Squeegee

Towel

Etching cream

Utensil for stirring etching cream

Handful of small glass beads (approximately five per glass) that complement your wineglasses (coordinate colors if you're using colored glass, as we have here) and fit on your wire

Safety glasses

Etching liquid

Plastic container

Plastic or wooden spoon

Approximately 6 inches (15 cm) of 16-gauge craft wire per glass (Craft and beading stores carry both sterling silver and tinned copper wire; choose whatever suits the color and style of your glasses best.)

Scissors or wire cutters

Round-nose pliers

1 Transfer the stencil pattern to the self-adhesive vinyl (making one copy for each glass in your set). Cut fringe lines into the vinyl around the design, then peel off the vinyl backing and apply the stencil to the glass. Fringing the stencil makes it easier to form it to the compound curves of the glass.

2 Use your craft knife equipped with a swivel blade to cut out the design on the glass, and a straight blade or pick-out tool to remove the cutout pieces. When removing pieces, always work from the center of the piece you're removing, not the edges, so you don't risk ruining your clean-cut lines.

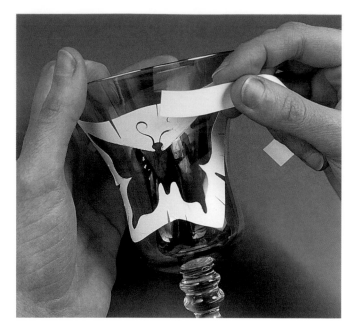

3 Cover the stencil with a scrap of self-adhesive vinyl backing, and squeegee over it to remove any air bubbles and press it firmly in place. With a slightly moistened cotton swab, clean up any adhesive residue the vinyl left behind. Use strips of vinyl to cover over the fringed edges of your stencil, making the strips wide enough so that you can pinch the corners and form a well around the design.

5 Wearing safety glasses to protect your eyes from any splashing, pour some etching liquid into a plastic container, and test one of your beads for etching time. (Some small beads may need as little as five minutes to etch to your satisfaction; others may take up to 15 minutes. Also, if you're working with beads that have a finish, such as the aurora borealis finish on the beads in this project, leaving them in the liquid too long may remove too much of the finish.) Once you've got the timing down, add about half of your beads to the liquid and stir them around so that all bead surfaces are well covered. Leave them in the liquid for the amount of time you determined, then pour off the liquid and rinse and dry the beads.

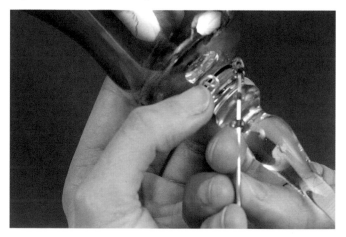

4 Nestle your glass in a towel, stir the etching cream, pour it out onto one of the vinyl edges, and use the squeegee to pull it quickly and evenly across the stencil. Leave the cream in place for the amount of time the manufacturer recommends. Scrape off the excess cream with the squeegee, and remove the stencil as you rinse the glass with water. Dry the glass. Repeat steps 1 through 4 for each of the glasses in your set.

6 Cut a piece of wire approximately 6 inches (15 cm) long. Make a small curve on one end with the round-nose pliers, add several beads from the other end (alternating etched and unetched beads), then curve the second end. With your fingers, curve the beaded wire around the stem of the wineglass, mirroring the curve in the butterfly's antennae, if you like. Repeat this step for each glass.

Celtic Knot Table

Ancient Celtic artisans used intertwining geometric patterns to decorate the surfaces of everything from household objects and ritual vessels to weapons and body ornaments. The strong symbols are just as striking today, and a flat glass tabletop is the perfect place to etch one.

2 Trim the edges of the vinyl around the straight lines
you marked, so the stencil will be easier to place.
Apply the stencil, starting on one side, peeling the
backing as you go, and smoothing the stencil down
with the squeegee as you work toward the other side. As
you work, line up the lines you marked with the edges
of the glass. Cover the stencil with the backing paper
you removed, and squeegee over it to make sure the
stencil is firmly attached and free of air bubbles.

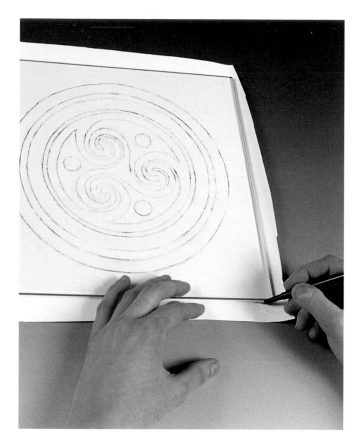

1 Cut a piece of self-adhesive vinyl slightly larger than
your glass tabletop. Using carbon paper and a
ballpoint pen, transfer the stencil to the vinyl. Center
the image under the glass tabletop, and lightly mark
straight lines around the stencil that correspond with
the edges of your tabletop.

3 With the swivel blade and/or the straight blade, carefully cut out the stencil. To remove inside pieces, be sure to use the picking technique, described on page 14, rather than attempting to gouge the pieces out from the side, which can destroy the sharp, clean edges you want. When you finish, rub off any adhesive residue the vinyl left behind.

4 Apply 1½- to 2-inch (3.8 to 5 cm) extension strips of self-adhesive vinyl along all the borders of your stencil, stir the etching cream, and pour a generous amount in a line along one of the extension strips. With the squeegee, spread the cream quickly and evenly over the entire stencil. Leave the cream in place for the amount of time the manufacturer recommends, scrape it off with the squeegee, and remove the stencil as you rinse the tabletop with water. Dry the tabletop.

Tip

The Celtic knot stencil we've provided for this project is reversible, so you can place your etched tabletop back in its table frame with the etched surface on top or showing through from the underside. We recommend you position it so the etched surface is on the underside. Not only will the tabletop be easier to clean, but the design will have added depth.

Herbed Oil & Vinegar Bottles

There's nothing new about sticking an herb sprig in a bottle of vinegar and calling it a personalized gift. If you haven't made one yourself, you've surely received one. But etching the outside of a bottle with a print that hints at the flavoring inside, now there's a tasteful twist on an old idea!

WHAT YOU NEED

Bottle of herbal oil or vinegar with flat panels, well sealed (If you're using a purchased bottle of oil or vinegar that features decorative tags, carefully remove the tags before beginning the project, then tie them back in place when you're finished.)

Plain paper

Ruler

Ballpoint pen

Carbon paper

Self-adhesive vinyl

Squeegee

Cotton swabs

Craft knife

Herb sprigs (Choose an herb that is neither too brittle nor too moist. You also want one that is relatively flat on one side. For best results, press the sprigs in a heavy book for a couple of days before using them.)

Adhesive spray

Etching cream

Utensil for stirring etching cream

2 Lay some of the herb sprigs on a piece of plain paper or newspaper and spray their flattest sides with adhesive.

1 Determine the size of the square or rectangle you want to etch on each of your bottle's four panels. Draw your square or rectangle stencil on the plain sheet of paper, transfer four copies to self-adhesive vinyl, and cut them out, leaving a border of approximately 2 inches (5 cm) around each. Take care not to overcut at the corners; if you do, you'll create slits in the stencil where etching cream could seep. Apply one of the stencils to the bottle panel you'll be working on first, lay a scrap of vinyl backing on top of it, and squeegee over the stencil to make sure it's firmly in place and all the corners are well sealed. Pinch the edges of the vinyl to form a well around the open area of the stencil. If necessary, use a moistened cotton swab to remove any adhesive residue.

3 Press the sprigs in place inside the square or rectangle stencil. Cover them with a scrap of vinyl backing and apply additional pressure to make sure they're firmly in place, then use another moistened cotton swab to clean up any adhesive residue around the sprigs. (Any leftover residue may prevent the etching cream from taking effect in those spots.)

4 Stir the etching cream, pour a generous amount onto the stencil border, then use the squeegee to pull it quickly and evenly over the area to be etched. Leave the cream in place for the amount of time the manufacturer recommends. Scrape off the excess cream with the squeegee, and remove the stencil and the herb sprigs as you rinse the bottle with water. Dry the bottle well, then repeat steps 1 through 4 on the other three panels.

Snowflake Ornaments

These radiant ornaments covered with glistening ice crystals require little more than squeezing on a series of lines and dots. (You can even follow one of the simple patterns we provide, if you like.) They're a perfect project for kids and first-time etchers. Get a group together, load up some applicator bottles, and have a ball!

WHAT YOU NEED
Snowflake Ornament patterns, page 76, to follow as a guide
Etching cream in an applicator bottle
Resist gel in an applicator bottle
Scrap paper
Plain glass ornaments in various sizes
Towel
Etching liquid
Plastic container
Safety glasses
Latex gloves

■ ■ ■

Variations:

You can create two different versions of these striking ornaments. For an etched snowflake on a clear glass ball, draw your design with etching cream, let it sit for the recommended amount of time, then rinse and dry the ornament. For a clear design on an etched ball, draw the design with resist gel, then dip the ball in etching liquid. The following photos demonstrate the second technique.

■ ■ ■

Tip

Because etching cream and resist gel are different consistencies, the same size tip will produce different size lines with each. Be sure to take this into consideration when you're testing tips.

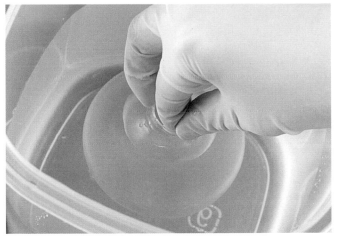

1 Using the patterns as a guide, experiment with squeezing out your freehand designs on a piece of scrap paper. In addition, test various tips on your applicator bottles to see what size lines they produce. (You'll probably want thinner lines for smaller ornaments and thicker lines for larger ones.) Once you're satisfied with your line size and you're comfortable squeezing out the design, begin applying the etching cream or resist gel to the surface of an ornament.

3 Wearing safety glasses, fill your plastic container with etching liquid. Remove the ornament's metal holder, and fill it partially with water to give it some weight and to stop any etching action if etching liquid gets inside the ornament. Dry the outside of the ornament completely. Put on latex gloves, hold the ornament by its tip, and dip the ornament slowly into the etching liquid, lowering it as far as possible without getting etching liquid inside the ornament. (On the finished ornament, the metal clasp will cover any unetched portion of the tip.) Hold the ornament in the liquid for the 10 or 15 minutes the manufacturer recommends. (You may want to have a good conversationalist or an interesting book nearby to help you through this part of the process!).

2 Draw the center of the design, then work outward, adding lines and dots according to the pattern you're following. If you're working with etching cream, leave the cream in place for the amount of time the manufacturer recommends, then rinse and dry the ornament. If you're working with resist gel, as we are here, let it dry until it's clear (probably several hours), and move on to the next step.

4 Remove the ornament from the liquid, rinse off the resist gel, and dry the ornament. If your etching liquid is reusable, pour it back into its original container.

Teacups

If you've got the idea that etched glass must always look sophisticated and serious, think again. Here, bright patches of paint accent the etching, adding just the right touch of playfulness. Any type of paint will adhere to your etched surface. We used craft paints specially designed for painting on glass, so the design is durable and safe for coming in contact with food.

WHAT YOU NEED

Oversized teacups

Teacups stencil pattern, page 76, sized on a photocopy machine to fit your cups

Self-adhesive vinyl

Carbon paper

Ballpoint pen

Craft knife with swivel blade

Squeegee

Etching creme

Utensils for stirring etching cream and paints

Opaque acrylic enamel paint for glass in red, blue, and yellow

Small or medium round artist's brush

Small rinse cup for brush

Cotton swabs (optional)

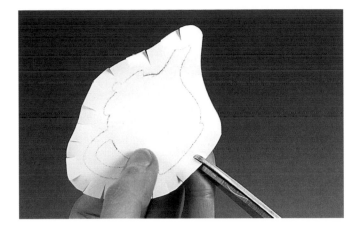

1 With carbon paper and a ballpoint pen, transfer three copies per cup of the teapot pattern to self-adhesive vinyl. Fringe the border around the stencils and cut an X in the center of each teapot shape, so you can more easily apply the stencils to the curved surface of the teacup.

2 Apply the stencils, spaced evenly, to the cup, and use a swivel blade to cut out the teapot shapes. Fill in between each stencil with strips of vinyl. Cover each stencil with a scrap of vinyl backing, and run the squeegee over it to make sure it's firmly in place. Remove any adhesive residue the vinyl left behind.

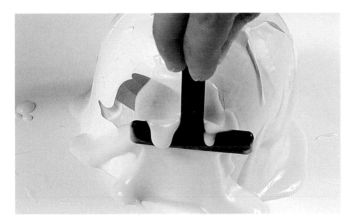

3 Mask the inside lip of the teacup with at least 1 inch (2.5 cm) of self-adhesive vinyl, and mask the rest of the cup, including the bottom, with scraps of vinyl. Turn the cup upside down on a sheet of vinyl. Stir the etching cream, pour some onto the vinyl base around the cup, and use the squeegee to pull it up over all three stencils. Leave the cream in place for the amount of time the cream manufacturer recommends, scrape it off, and remove the stencil as you rinse the cup with water. Dry the cup.

4 Stir the glass paints before using them, and follow any other manufacturer instructions for their use. Paint the spout of one of the etched teapots blue.

5 Add a red lid to the second teapot and a yellow handle to the third, cleaning the brush each time you switch paint colors. You can use a lightly moistened cotton swab to remove any small spots of paint that end up where you don't want them. Cure the paint according to the manufacturer's instructions (the process may require brief oven baking).

Drawer Pulls

The contents of the drawer may be tiresomely ordinary. Dental floss and vitamins, maybe. Or unorganized office supplies. Or socks. But add a dash of unexpected glamour to the knobs on the outside, and everyone will imagine it's full of neat stacks of imported linens and collections of hand-milled soap.

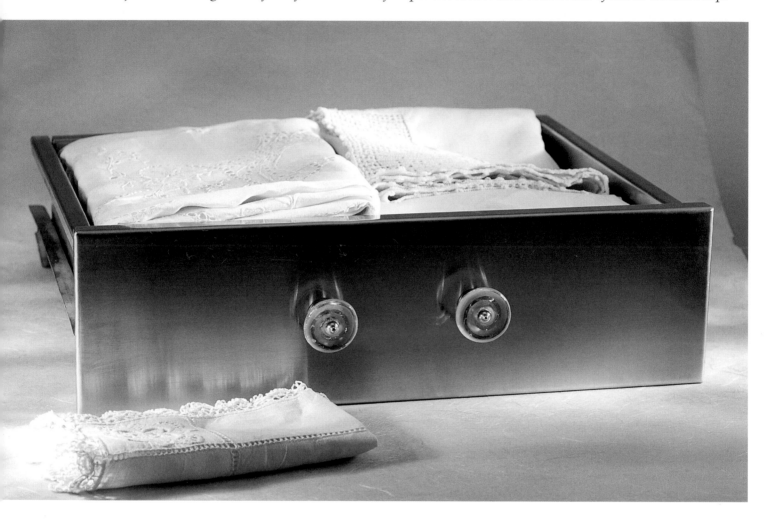

WHAT YOU NEED

Round glass drawer pulls

Resist gel in applicator bottle with large tip

Cotton swabs

Empty bottle with small opening (such as a vanilla extract bottle)

Etching liquid

Plastic container

Safety glasses

Wooden or plastic spoon

1 Squeeze out a thin spiral of resist gel on the front of the drawer pull, beginning at the outside edge of the drawer pull and moving toward the center. Keep the applicator tip approximately ⅛ to ¼ inch (3 to 6 mm) above the glass as you squeeze out the gel, holding the bottle at an angle and moving it ahead of where you're laying down your line. (You can use the pattern on page 76 as a guide for practicing first, if you like. Make several copies and experiment with tracing over them. Also, if you wind up with a spiral on your actual drawer pull that you simply can't live with, you can clean off any crooked lines or other small mistakes with a moistened cotton swab—or, rinse off the entire piece and start over.)

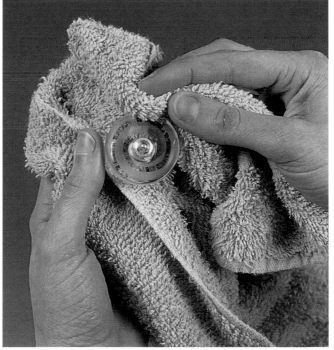

3 Wearing safety glasses, pour enough etching liquid into your plastic container to cover the drawer pulls. Place them in the liquid, and move them gently with the spoon to ensure good coverage of the pieces.

2 Cover the entire back of the drawer pull with resist gel (so that it will remain clear after you've etched the piece). Prop the drawer pull on the bottle with a small opening, with only the metal portion of the drawer pull coming into contact with the bottle, and let the resist gel dry clear (probably overnight). Repeat steps 1 and 2 on your other drawer pulls.

4 After the amount of time the etching liquid manufacturer recommends, pour off the liquid (pouring it back into its original container if it's reusable), wipe off the gel while rinsing the drawer pulls, and dry them.

Door Frames

This bold design of connecting curves could easily be adapted to any series of vertical windows that need a bit of dressing up.

WHAT YOU NEED

Pair of door frames, each with three vertical windows

Three copies of each version of the Door Frames stencil pattern, page 76, sized on a photocopy machine to fit the windows in your frames (One version of the pattern is designed for your left door frame; the other is for the right.)

Carbon paper

Ballpoint pen

Self-adhesive vinyl

Tape

Scissors

Squeegee

Etching cream

Utensil for stirring etching cream

Tip

We recommend you etch on the inside surface of your window panels. That way, the design has added depth when it's viewed from outside, and the etched surface won't be exposed to outside elements. Also, we're working on frames that have not yet been installed, but you could just as easily etch the windows of frames that are already in place on each side of your door.

1 Make two vinyl copies of each version of the stencil pattern, transferring the patterns to self-adhesive vinyl with carbon paper and a ballpoint pen. Beginning with the top window of the left frame, tape your sized photocopy of the left-frame stencil pattern to the outside surface of the window, so it shows through in its proper position on the inside.

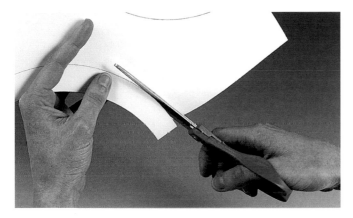

2 Cut out one of the left-frame vinyl stencils.

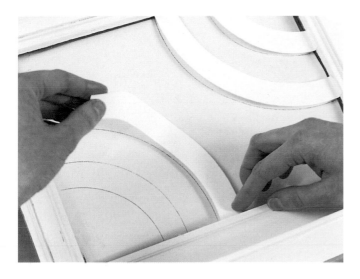

3 Attach the appropriate stencil pieces (the thin, inner strips of the design) to the inside of the window panel. The project photo illustrates which areas should be masked from the etching cream, and the taped pattern on the other side of the glass helps with placement.

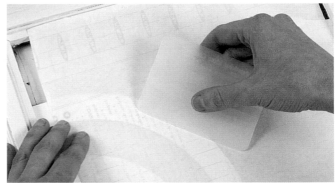

4 Cover the attached masking pieces with a scrap of vinyl backing, and run the squeegee over them to ensure that they're firmly in place. Cut a large piece of vinyl (about the size of your window). Stir the etching cream, pour a generous amount on the vinyl piece you cut, hold it close to the window, and use the squeegee to pull the cream from the vinyl quickly and evenly over the window panel.

5 Leave the cream in place for the amount of time the manufacturer recommends, then scrape as much of it off as possible. Rinse the rest off with water and a sponge before you remove the stencil, then rinse with a sponge as you remove the stencil. Dry the window. Repeat the process on all the other window panels, reversing your stencil pieces as you move down each frame. (For example, on the middle left window, you'll use the large, fat masking pieces you cut out but didn't use on the top window. On the bottom left window, you'll need to cut out your second left-frame vinyl stencil and use the same masking pieces you used on the top window.)

Breakfast Place Setting

There's no getting around it; tableware is meant to hold food and drink. That means you probably don't want to decorate it with a fussy pattern that'll compete with what's inside or on top of it. Here's a simple, sharp checkerboard design that's perfect for accenting a place setting without taking over.

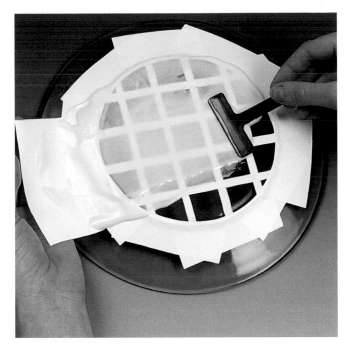

PLATE

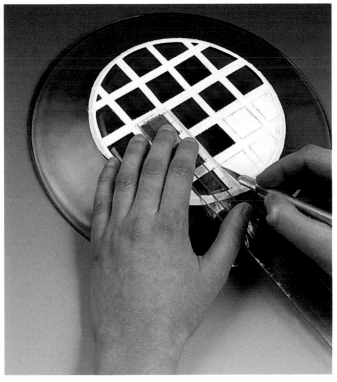

2 Once your stencil is completely cut out, lay the backing from the self-adhesive vinyl on top of it and run the squeegee over the stencil, pressing it firmly in place. Wipe off any adhesive residue on the glass surface. Extend the edges of the stencil by adding strips of self-adhesive vinyl, then pinch the edges together to form a well around the stencil, to prevent the etching cream from dripping down the sides of the plate. Stir the etching cream, pour it onto one of the vinyl edges, spread it quickly and evenly over the entire stencil with the squeegee, and leave it in place for the amount of time the manufacturer recommends. Scrape off the excess cream with the squeegee, and remove the stencil as you rinse the plate with water. Dry the plate.

1 Transfer the plate pattern to self-adhesive vinyl, then center the vinyl pattern and apply it to the back side of the center of the plate. With the craft knife, carefully cut out the squares in the stencil. If you overcut on any of the corners, patch the slit tightly with a small scrap of vinyl so etching cream won't seep into it.

BOWL

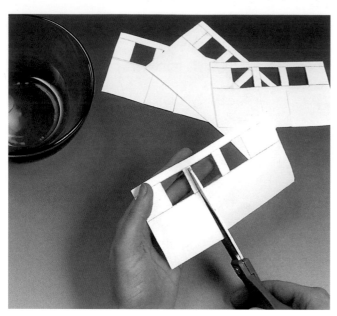

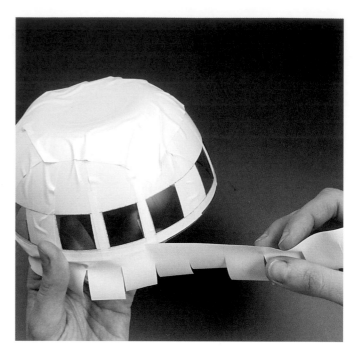

1 Transfer four copies of the bowl/mug pattern to self-adhesive vinyl. Cut out each copy, then use the ruler and craft knife to cut out the square shapes, so you end up with four intact strips of three squares. Cut along the dotted lines between each square.

3 Apply self-adhesive vinyl around the lip and rim of the bowl, inside the rim of the bowl (covering at least 1 inch [2.5 cm] of the inside surface), and, in a patched fashion, around the bottom of the bowl. Turn the bowl upside down and apply a vinyl "skirt."

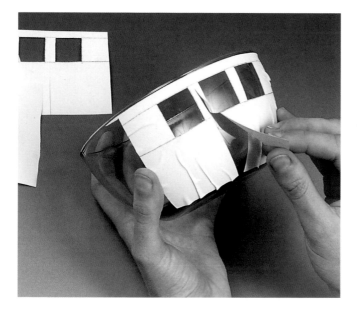

2 Apply the first of your four strips, laying it down just below the rim of the bowl. Attach the two outer squares on the strip first, then lay down the middle one, so it fits the curve of the bowl and is evenly spaced between the two outer squares. Apply the second strip in the same way on the opposite side of the bowl. Apply the other two strips opposite each other, so all four strips are evenly spaced.

4 Pour etching cream onto the skirt, all the way around the bowl, and use the squeegee to pull the cream evenly up over the stencil areas. Leave the cream in place for the amount of time the manufacturer recommends. Scrape off the excess cream with the squeegee, and remove the stencil as you rinse the bowl under water. Dry the bowl.

You'll use the same process for etching the mug, with one exception: apply only two strips of squares evenly around the rim, rather than four.

Champagne Flutes

When was the last time your empty champagne glass came outfitted with its very own bubbles? If you're looking for a reason for a party, these spirited flutes are it. Oh, and one more thing to celebrate: this ranks among the easiest projects in the book!

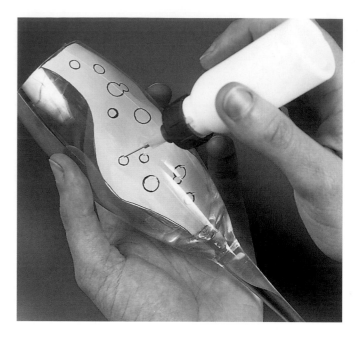

2 Screw a small tip on the bottle of resist gel. Following the pattern, trace the small, arched, reflection curve inside each bubble. Let the resist gel dry until it's clear (which should probably take less than an hour).

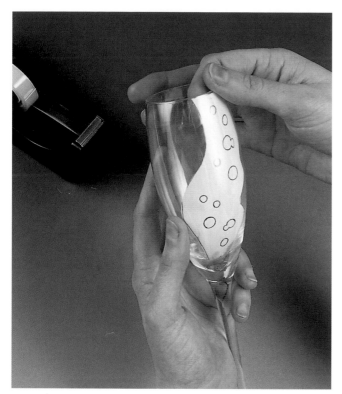

1 Arrange your sized pattern on the inside of your glass, so the bubbles show through where you want them to be, then tape the pattern in place.

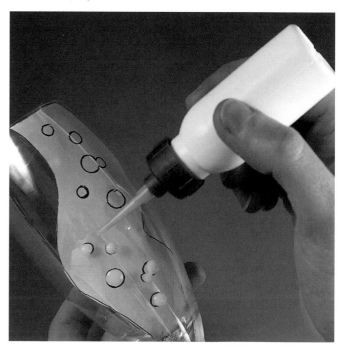

3 Add a large tip to the bottle of etching cream. Hold the bottle in a vertical position, with the tip poised in the middle of a bubble, and squeeze out a dot of cream large enough to cover the resist-gel reflection mark and to extend to the edges of the circle on the pattern. Repeat the process of applying etching cream to all of the bubble spots.

4 Leave the cream in place for the amount of time the manufacturer recommends, then remove the pattern from the inside of the glass, rinse the glass with water, and dry it. Repeat steps 1 through 4 on all the glasses in your set.

Tip

If you're working on glass with a coating, like the iridescent one on the flutes shown here, the vapors from the etching cream may eat away some of the nearby coating. To prevent that, you can add a ring of resist gel around the bubble spots and let it dry before applying the dots of etching cream. Or, you might experiment with leaving your cream on for a shorter amount of time.

Hurricane Lamp

Covering large surfaces evenly can be a challenge when you're etching glass with cream. Sponging offers a clever solution and creates a soft, mottled finish that's perfect for filtering light from a lamp. A bit of gold outliner added at the end can set off your design—and set everything aglow.

WHAT YOU NEED

Hurricane Lamp leaf pattern, page 77, sized on a photocopy machine so it suits your piece (The leaves on our project are approximately 6 inches [15 cm] long.)

Ballpoint pen

Carbon paper

Self-adhesive vinyl

Scissors

Hurricane lamp

Scrap piece of vinyl backing

Squeegee

Etching cream

Utensil for stirring etching cream

Flat plastic dish or lid

Dry sponge (We used a natural sea sponge. Different sponges create different textures; experiment and choose one you like.)

Gold outliner for painting on glass

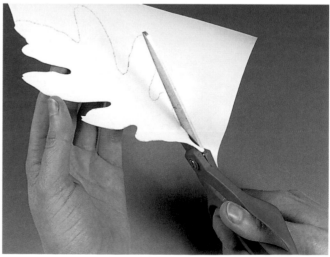

1 Use the carbon paper and pen to transfer the leaf pattern six times to a piece of self-adhesive vinyl. Cut the leaves out of the vinyl with scissors.

cream's effect). You may also want to experiment first on a piece of practice glass to determine what level of coverage appeals to you once the glass is rinsed and dried. When you're satisfied, sponge over the outside of the entire hurricane in an up-and-down motion, being careful not to smear the cream on with the sponge. Leave the cream in place for the amount of time the manufacturer recommends, and remove the vinyl as you rinse it with water. Dry the hurricane lamp.

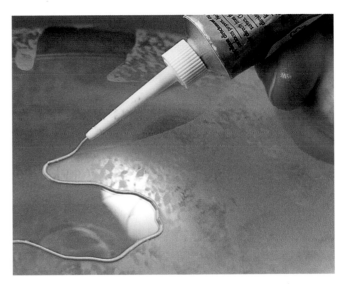

2 Stick the leaves to the surface of the hurricane lamp in a random arrangement, starting at the stem of each leaf, and peeling and sticking as you move up the leaf shape. Cover each with a scrap of vinyl backing, and squeegee over it to make sure the vinyl is firmly in place. Because you're working on a curved surface, you might also have to use your fingers to press the leaves in place. Remove any adhesive residue. Also, apply strips of vinyl to the inside rim of both the top and bottom of the hurricane lamp to protect those areas from any stray etching cream. You may need to fringe the strips to get them to adhere well to the curved shape of the rims.

4 Outline the leaf shapes with gold outliner, applying it directly from the tube. Keep the tube's tip approximately ¼ inch (6 mm) above the glass, apply even pressure, and let the paint line fall onto the glass. Fill any large etched areas with simple spirals of outliner, using the same technique, if you like. Follow the outliner manufacturer's directions for curing the paint.

3 Stir the etching cream, then pour some into the plastic container. Before you begin sponging on the hurricane lamp, make sure your sponge is completely dry (water will interfere with the etching

Tip

When you're applying etching cream with an applicator bottle, keep a few cotton swabs and a plastic cup of water nearby. Since water stops the effect of etching cream, you can carefully swipe off small mistakes with a moistened swab.

Punch Bowl Set

Making a pretty set like this one is a piece of cake—and even easier than icing one.
Start with glassware that features a raised pattern, and the hard work of figuring out what
goes where is already taken care of. All you've got to do to bring the look to life is pipe etching cream
from an applicator bottle right along the lines.

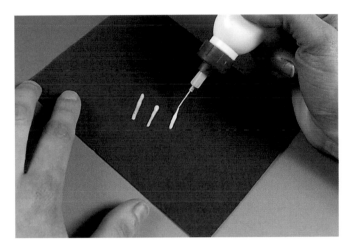

1 Stir the etching cream, pour it into an applicator bottle, attach a tip to the bottle, then test it by drawing a line of cream on a piece of paper or a paper towel. Depending on the raised design you're working with, you may want a tip that produces a thicker or thinner line of cream. If necessary, switch tips and keep experimenting until you find one that suits your project.

2 Begin applying etching cream to the design. In some cases, you may want to only outline the design. In others, you might choose to fill in design elements entirely. We've alternated the two approaches when etching the flowers and leaves on this set.

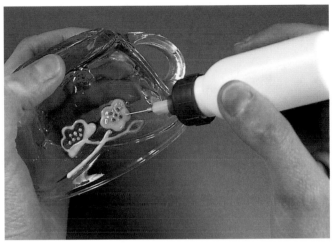

3 Note how long the etching cream you're using must be left on the glass, then keep your eye on the clock as you etch. Most etching creams need 15 minutes to take effect and can be left on your glass for up to 30 minutes. If that's the case, you can etch for 15 minutes, take a 15 minute break, rinse and dry the section you've completed, then start the process again. (The advantage of this technique is that you don't have to complete your punch bowl set in a single etching session. You can stop for a longer break after any 30-minute cycle.)

4 Once you've completed an entire piece, rinse it and dry it. When you finish a session, clean your applicator tip by attaching it to a bottle filled with warm water and squeezing the water through until the tip is free of cream.

Martini Set

Even a batch of add-water-and-stir pink lemonade would look sophisticated served in a set like this.
The maze of masking you've got to stick on to make it requires some careful attention to detail.
Just keep in mind that after all that work, you can fill up the results and celebrate.

Martini pitcher and glasses

Self-adhesive vinyl

Ruler

Craft knife

Scissors

Water-based permanent marker or china marker

Utensil for stirring etching cream

Etching cream

Squeegee

Plastic container

Water

Safety glasses

Etching liquid

Latex gloves

2 Mark four equidistant points around the rim of the glass and four other points on the inside of the glass at the base, each falling directly below one of the points on the rim.

MARTINI GLASS

1 Cut a strip of self-adhesive vinyl ¼ inch (6 mm) wide and long enough to wrap around where the base of the glass meets the stem. Use a ruler to make sure the edge that will be against the base of the glass is perfectly straight. With the scissors, fringe the other edge so it fits around the curve of the stem, then apply the strip. Once the strip is in place, cut several more strips ¼ to ½ inch (6 mm to 1.3 cm) wide, and apply them over the first strip to secure it and to provide additional masking of the the stem.

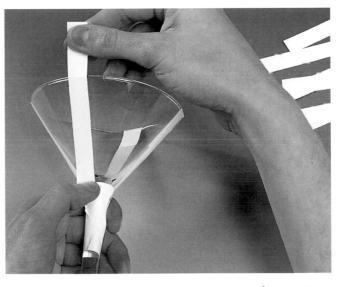

3 Cut four strips of vinyl, each measuring ½ inch (1.3 cm) wide and about 4 inches (10 cm) long. Apply them to the outside of the glass from dot to dot (connecting the dots vertically), so you create triangular openings that will be etched.

4 Cut additional pieces of vinyl to cover any open patches on the outside of the glass where you don't want etching cream to make contact (any places outside of the triangular areas). Cover the inside of the glass with a strip of vinyl at least 1 inch (2.5 cm) wide to protect the area in case any of the cream splatters or drips while you're etching the outside of the glass.

5 Turn the glass upside down and place it on a large piece of self-adhesive vinyl. Stir the cream, pour a generous amount onto the vinyl all the way around the rim of the glass, hold the glass steady by its base, and use the squeegee to pull the cream up onto the two exposed triangular areas, covering them quickly and evenly. Don't adjust the position of the glass once you've applied the cream; you'll risk getting cream inside the glass. Leave the cream in place for the amount of time the manufacturer recommends, scrape it off with the squeegee, and remove the vinyl as you rinse it with water. Dry the glass.

6 To dip the stem of the glass, first place the glass in a plastic container and fill the container with water to the level where the stem meets the base of the glass. Remove the glass, and mark the water level on the container. Dump out the water, and dry the glass and the container thoroughly. Wearing safety glasses to protect your eyes from any splashing, pour etching liquid into the container up to the marked level, place the stem in the liquid, allow it to sit in the liquid for the amount of time the manufacturer recommends, then pour the liquid back into the bottle (if it's reusable), and rinse and dry the glass. If you want to finish the bottom of the base (where air prevented the liquid from etching), apply a bit of etching cream with a gloved finger, leave it on for approximately five minutes, then rinse and dry the base.

MARTINI PITCHER

1 Determine the centerline of the pitcher and use dots to mark it. Apply a straight strip of vinyl ½ inch (1.3 cm) wide around the middle of the pitcher,

with the top edge of the strip along the dotted line and the rest of the strip extending onto the bottom half of the pitcher.

2 Mark four equidistant points around the rim of the pitcher, four corresponding points on the center line, and four corresponding points around the bottom of the pitcher. Apply straight strips of vinyl to connect the points on the rim with the points on the center line so that you form the borders for two open and equally sized rectangular areas. You're left with two other equally sized rectangular areas on the top of the pitcher that are partially filled in with the strips of vinyl. Mask them completely with scraps of vinyl. (In determining which rectangular areas will be etched and which will remain clear, pay attention to where your pitcher's spout and handle, if it has one, are. You'll want to make sure your clear rectangular areas include those two elements, so you don't have to etch them.) Cover the inside rim of the pitcher with strips of vinyl at least 1 inch (2.5 cm) wide to protect the area in case any of the cream splatters or drips while you're etching the outside of the pitcher.

3 With your fingernail, burnish each intersection where the vinyl strips overlap to ensure that the spots are firmly sealed.

4 Turn the pitcher upside down on a piece of self-adhesive vinyl. Stir the etching cream, pour a generous amount around the rim of the pitcher, and use the squeegee to pull it quickly and evenly over the open rectangular areas on the top half of the pitcher. Leave the cream in place for the amount of time the manufacturer recommends, scrape it off with the squeegee, and remove the vinyl as you rinse the pitcher with water. Dry the pitcher.

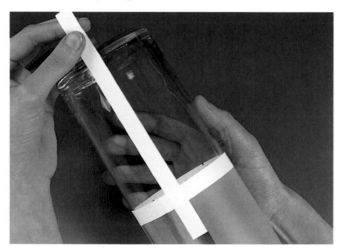

5 Repeat the process to etch the bottom half of the pitcher, but reverse the positions of your etched and unetched rectangles (so that you have clear rectangles below etched rectangles and vice versa). In addition, apply scraps of vinyl masking to the bottom of the pitcher for this step, so you protect it from the etching cream.

THIS CHARGER FEATURES A FREEHAND DESIGN CREATED WITH ETCHING CREAM APPLIED WITH AN APPLICATOR BOTTLE.

Designer: *Bob Bosler*

Photographer: *Brett Turner*

THIS SMALL PIN WAS ACID ETCHED ON DICHROIC GLASS.

Designer and photographer:

Jackie Paciello

Gallery of Etched Glass

On the following pages, we feature additional pieces that were etched with the same craft products and techniques described in this book. We also showcase others that were etched using more complicated acid or abrasive blasting techniques. We include this second category of pieces as a source of inspiration —and as examples of the range of possibilities for etching on glass.

THIS TIGER IMAGE WAS ETCHED WITH CREAM ON A MARBLE TILE.

Designer: *Bob Bosler*

PHOTOGRAPHER: *Brett Turner*

WITH RESIST GEL AND ETCHING LIQUID, THE DESIGNER CREATED A LAMP BASE THAT MATCHES THE SHADE.

DESIGNER: *Barb Bosler*

PHOTOGRAPHER: *Brett Turner*

FOR THIS HOLIDAY PLACE SETTING, THE DESIGNER USED ETCHING CREAM AND STENCILS TO REMOVE THE GLAZED FINISH FROM THE CERAMIC PIECES, LEAVING BEHIND A SMOOTH, WHITE DESIGN.

Designer: *Bob Bosler*

PHOTOGRAPHER: *Brett Turner*

THE DESIGNER ETCHED THIS FISH-SHAPED PLATTER WITH CREAM ON THE BACK SIDE, THEN LAYERED METAL COATINGS AND PATINAS OVER THE ETCHED SURFACE.

DESIGNER: *Margot A. Clark*

PHOTOGRAPHER: *Douglas Holder*

THE SURFACE OF THIS GLASS PLAQUE WAS ETCHED WITH LIQUID, THEN PAINTED WITH ACRYLIC PAINTS. THE PATINA COPPER INLAY WAS CREATED WITH LIQUID METAL COATINGS AND PATINAS.

DESIGNER: *Margot A. Clark*

PHOTOGRAPHER: *Douglas Holder*

RHINESTONES ARE SOLDERED
SURFACE OF THIS ACID-ETCHED DEC

DESIGNER: *Jackie Pa*

PHOTOGRAPHER: *MNM D*

**ACID-ETCHED DICHROIC GLASS, FUSED AND WRAPPED
WITH GOLD WIRE**

DESIGNER AND PHOTOGRAPHER: *Jackie Paciello*

**HERE, ETCHING CREAM WAS USED ON A CHINA PLATE TO PREPARE THE
SURFACE FOR AN ACRYLIC-PAINT DESIGN OF COLUMBINE AND IVY.**

DESIGNER AND PHOTOGRAPHER: *Rebecca Baer*

USING A SANDBLASTING TECHNIQUE, THE DESIGNER ETCHED
THE SILVERED SIDE OF THIS MIRROR PANEL,
WHICH ALLOWS LIGHT TO PASS THROUGH THE ETCHED AREAS.

DESIGNER: *Elaine C. Block*

PHOTOGRAPHER: *Lifestyle Photography*

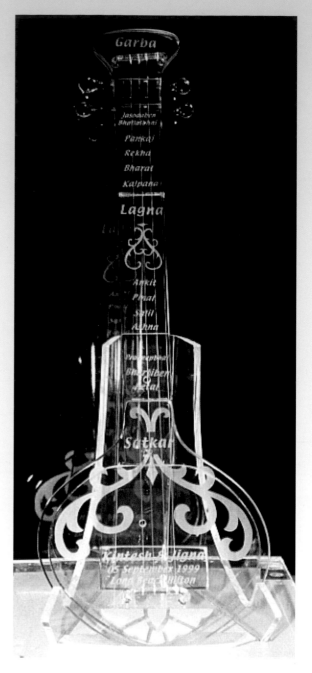

THIS HAND-CUT PIECE IN THE SHAPE OF AN INDIAN SITAR
FEATURES A SANDBLASTED DESIGN.

DESIGNER AND PHOTOGRAPHER: *Larry Cox*

ONE OF A SET OF TWO SIDELIGHT PANELS
FEATURING A SANDBLASTED FLORAL DESIGN

DESIGNER: *Elaine C. Block*

PHOTOGRAPHER: *Lifestyle Photography*

DETAIL OF A 21-FOOT-LONG (6.3 M) MULTILAYER GLASS CARVING

ENTITLED *FACES OF THE FOREST*

DESIGNER AND PHOTOGRAPHER: *Kathy Bradford*

THIS SANDBLASTED PANEL FEATURING A VICTORIAN DESIGN IS ONE OF A

SET OF FOUR CONNECTED PANELS DESIGNED

FOR A RESIDENTIAL ENTRYWAY.

DESIGNER: *Elaine C. Block*

PHOTOGRAPHER: *Lifestyle Photography*

THE MIRRORED PANEL ON THIS
BOX OF STAINED GLASS AND WOOD
WAS ETCHED WITH A STENCIL
AND CREAM.

DESIGNER AND PHOTOGRAPHER:
Lisa Murdock

THIS DECORATIVE BOTTLE FILLED WITH OLIVE OIL WAS DIPPED IN ETCHING LIQUID, THEN PAINTED WITH ACRYLIC PAINTS.

DESIGNER AND PHOTOGRAPHER :
Rebecca Baer

TO ETCH THESE LARGE SURFACES OF STOREFRONT GLASS, THE DESIGNER USED ETCHING CREAM APPLIED WITH A PLASTIC DUSTPAN AS A SQUEEGEE.

Designer: *Bob Bosler*

PHOTOGRAPHER: *Brett Turner*

A REVERSE-ETCHED BAMBOO DESIGN DECORATES THIS WINDOW PANEL, ONE OF A SET OF SIX PANELS ALL ETCHED BY SANDBLASTING.

DESIGNER: *Elaine C. Block*

PHOTOGRAPHER: *Lifestyle Photography*

A WINDOW ETCHED BY SANDBLASTING

DESIGNER AND PHOTOGRAPHER: *Kathy Bradford*

GLASS CARVING, A MORE SOPHISTICATED PROCESS
THAN SURFACE ETCHING, IS USED TO CREATE THREE-
DIMENSIONAL DESIGNS IN WHICH THE ELEMENTS OF
THE DESIGN ARE BLASTED AT DIFFERENT DEPTHS. THIS
PIECE, ENTITLED *LOBOS DE LA LUNA*, IS AN EXQUISITE
EXAMPLE OF THE TECHNIQUE.

DESIGNER AND PHOTOGRAPHER: *Kathy Bradford*

CANDLESTICKS AND BEADS ETCHED WITH
ETCHING LIQUID

Designer: *Bob Bosler*

PHOTOGRAPHER: *Brett Turner*

Etching Glass Gallery **73**

PATTERNS

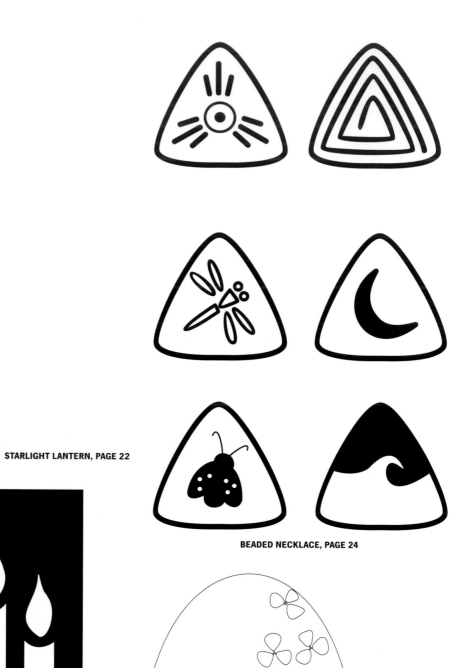

STARLIGHT LANTERN, PAGE 22

BEADED NECKLACE, PAGE 24

OIL LAMP, PAGE 28

BRUSHED PLATTER, PAGE 30

WINEGLASSES WITH BUTTERFLIES AND BEADS, PAGE 36

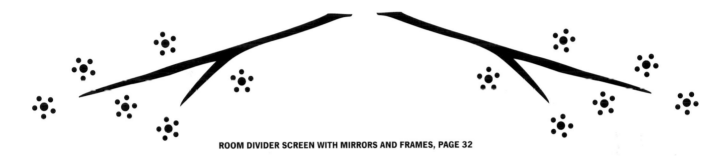

ROOM DIVIDER SCREEN WITH MIRRORS AND FRAMES, PAGE 32

CELTIC KNOT TABLE, PAGE 39

PATTERNS

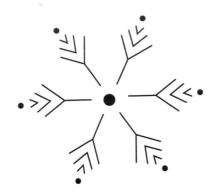

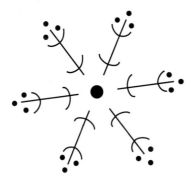

SNOWFLAKE ORNAMENTS, PAGE 44

TEACUPS, PAGE 46

DRAWER PULLS, PAGE 48

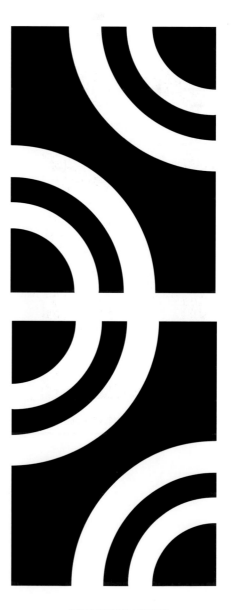

DOOR FRAMES, PAGE 50

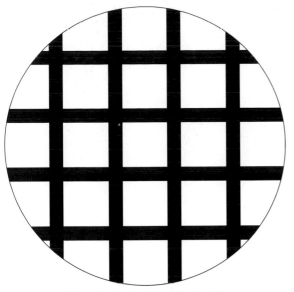

BREAKFAST PLACE SETTING: PLATE, PAGE 52

HURRICANE LAMP, PAGE 58

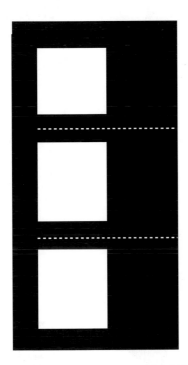

BREAKFAST PLACE SETTING: BOWL/MUG, PAGE 52

CHAMPAGNE FLUTES, PAGE 55

Contributors

Project Designer **DIANA LIGHT** is an accomplished artisan who specializes in painted and etched glass pieces, as well as oil and watercolor creations. She paints commissioned pieces for clients and sells her work through her Blue Light Boutique in Weaverville, North Carolina. Visit the boutique's website at www.angelfire.com/NC2/diana/bluelight.html.

GALLERY ARTISTS

REBECCA BAER, certified craft designer, publishes a variety of elegant pattern packets for the heirloom painter. They're available at decorative painting shops, trade shows, and through her website: www.rebeccabaer.com.

MICHAEL K. AND ELAINE C. BLOCK operate Delicate Touch Custom Etching in Oswego, Illinois. They use a sandblast etching technique to create custom-designed architectural pieces for both residences and businesses, and often pair their etched pieces with stained glass.

BARB BOSLER, known as the "Etching Lady," has always been fascinated by glass and mirrors. She is a member of the Society of Craft Designers and of Tole and Decorative Painters, as well as a Professional Demonstrator for Hobby Industry Association and a Priscilla Hauser Accredited Teacher. With these credentials, she teaches and gives seminars all over the world.

BOB BOSLER creates custom stencils and markets etched storefronts, which he creates by etching vertically with etching cream. You can view additional examples of his work by visiting his website: www.etchall.com.

KATHY BRADFORD creates site-specific architectural installations using sandcarving and etching techniques. All of her custom pieces are one of a kind.

MARGOT A. CLARK, an author, teacher, and designer, teaches etched glass and liquid metal techniques in the United States, Canada, and Europe.

LARRY COX, through his company, Glass Tattoo, has been designing, building, and installing custom art glass for more than 25 years. He uses several techniques to incorporate neon lighting, airbrushing, painting, custom glue chipping, wheel cutting, and chemical etching into his sandblasted and carved pieces.

LISA MURDOCK creates and markets original art glass windows and objects through her business, Custom Designed Stained Glass, in Virginia Beach, Virginia.

JACKIE PACIELLO, of Oak Lawn, Illinois, creates and sells her line of Celtic jewelry, along with wire-sculpted dichroic and natural stone jewelry, at Bristol Renaissance Faire and various other art shows throughout the year.

Acknowledgments

A number of generous people contributed time, talent, and their wares to help make this book complete. Special thanks to: Barb Bosler, of etchall glass etching products, for graciously sharing expertise, contacts, and lots of supplies; Susan J. Henshall of Armour Products, and Angela Scherz of Pebeo, who contributed products; Blue Mountain Candle Company and Mountain Lights, both of Asheville, North Carolina, for helping set several of the projects aglow; and Robin, Ivo, Lucy, and Django at Preservation Hall in Asheville, North Carolina, for contributing the door frames for the project on page 50.

In addition, the designer would like to personally thank Malcolm, who served as a patient and dedicated creative consultant throughout her work on the book; Tania, Heather, Karen, and Forrest; her friends and family; and Paige ("awesome editor") and all the folks at Lark Books.

INDEX

Applicator bottles and tips, 10

Building a well, 16

Colored glass, etching on, 10

Craft knives, 11

Embellishing etched glass, 18

Etching creams and liquids, 8

Etching liquid, dipping with, 17

Etching cream, applying, 15

Extension strips, 16

Flat glass, etching on, 9

Found-object resists, applying, 15

Found-object resists, 9

Fringing stencils, 15

Glass with a raised pattern, etching on, 10

Glass with simple curves, etching on, 9

Glass with compound curves, etching on, 10

Painting combined with etching, 19

Picking technique for removing stencils, 14

Resist gel, 9

Resist gel, applying, 16

Resists, 8

Safety equipment, 12

Self-adhesive vinyl resists, 8

Self-adhesive vinyl resists, applying, 15

Squeegees, 10

Stamping combined with etching, 19

Stencils as resists, 8

Stencils, applying, 14

Stencils, making, 13

Stencils, cutting techniques, 13

Textured glass, etching on, 10